SOCIAL OUTLOOK

Akiko Miyama **Junko Murao**

はじめに

　元号が「平成」から「令和」に変わり、日本では超高齢社会の先駆けとして、政府が「人生100年時代」を見据えた経済社会システムの大改革に本格的に取り組もうとしています。近未来社会では、社会・経済・医療・文化・環境などあらゆる分野で「モノのインターネット（IoT）」化が急速に進み、超高齢社会を支えていくことになるでしょう。一方、世界では、この IoT 時代を支える次世代 5G 通信の覇権争いが中国とアメリカのあいだで勃発しています。目まぐるしく変化する世界の最先端情報に絶えず目配りするグローバル人材が今ほど必要とされているときはありません。

　本書では、英字新聞やインターネットから興味深い英文素材を取り上げていますが、生きた英語に触れると共に、グローバル化に対応できる、情報の要点を即座に把握できる速読・速聴能力を養えるような設問内容となっています。また、何度もメディアで取り上げられているような話題を選択していますので、話題そのものにも関心を持つことができ、関連情報を手に入れようという姿勢も養えます。

本書の使い方

　さて、当テキストの具体的構成ですが、**Warm-up**、**Reading**、**Comprehension**、**Further Activity** の 4 セクションからなっています。以下に、具体的に各セクションのねらいや学習法を説明していますので、本章使用の際に参考にしてください。

　まず、**Warm-up** では、TOEIC® L&R テストなどの英語資格試験のための基礎力を養うべく、速聴・速読用の設問形式にしています。

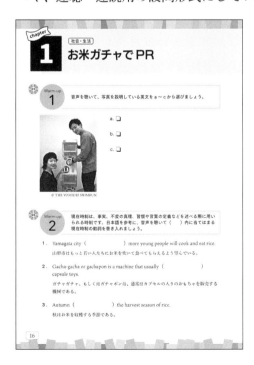

Warm-up 1

　TOEIC® テストの Part 1 の形式で、写真やイラストやグラフなどの視覚情報を利用して、章で扱っている**トピックのイメージを把握**します。後のセクションの背景知識を構築する大切なセクションです。

Warm-up 2

　語や句レベルのリスニング力を養うセクションです。発音規則や簡単な文法をリスニング形式の問題を通して学習します。このセクションで扱う語彙は、**後続セクションの重要表現**にもなっていますので、解答するだけでなく、しっかり覚えるようにしましょう。

Warm-up 3

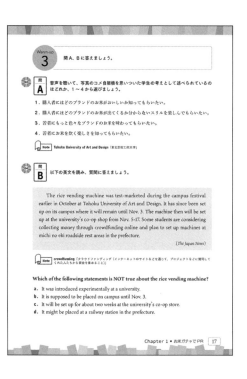

　背景知識を構築するための**リスニング**の練習問題（問Ａ）と、短い記事を用いた**拾い読み**の練習問題（問Ｂ）です。できるだけ辞書を引かずに、**速読・速聴**するように心がけてください。細部が聞き取れなくても、読み取れなくても、それが気にならない姿勢を養いましょう。そうすることで、長い英文を読んだり、聴いたりする場合の抵抗感がなくなります。

Reading

　色々な分野のトピックが選択されていますので、興味深く英語学習を続けることができるはずです。このセクションも、できる限り辞書に頼らず、**Warm-up** のセクションで培った背景知識をもとに推理力を働かせて読む癖をつけ、実社会で役立つ、**要点を把握しながら速読する**力を養うように心がけてください。難解な表現には注（Notes）を付けていますが、分からない表現が出てきたら、すぐ注を参照するのではなく、**あらかじめ意味を類推してから注で確認する**という読み方をしてください。

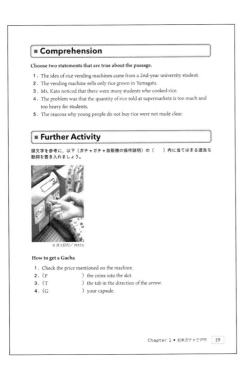

Comprehension

　Reading セクションの**内容理解を確認する**セクションです。長文が苦手な人は、先にこのセクションに目を通し、**Reading** の内容を予測するのもよいでしょう。**Reading** のセクションは、逐語訳しないで、当セクションの答えを探すという**拾い読み**をすることで、**速読力を養う**ことができます。

Further Activity

　章のトピックに関連した、さまざまなジャンルの英文素材を取り上げています。このセクションは、**速読、類推力**を試す問題になっていますので、辞書には頼らず、スピーディーな解答を心がけてください。

　当テキスト全章を学んだ後では、どんなニュースを目にしても、テキストで学習した手法を用いて、無意識にウォーム・アップがなされ、重要情報を素早く読み取る力が養われていることでしょう。

著者

CONTENTS

英字新聞の読み方

　英字新聞記事は、「ヘッドライン（見出し）」「リード（書き出し）」「ボディー（本文）」のパートからなり、読者が短時間で必要な情報を手に入れることができるように、さまざまな工夫がなされています。どんな工夫があるか、各パート別に見てみましょう。

A　ヘッドライン

　ヘッドラインは、ニュースを最も簡潔に伝えるという役割を担っていて、そのため思い切った省略や工夫が慣例的になされており、それを心得ていることが肝要です。また、ヘッドラインは読者を引きつける広告のような役割も果たしていますので、短いだけではなく、しばしば読者が魅力を感じるような表現の工夫もなされています。 次に、その慣例の特徴をまとめ、それらの特徴を含んだヘッドラインを例示しました。

1　時制の用法

a. 過去・現在完了は現在形で表す。

Internet beats TV among Japanese people in their 40s

　ある調査によると、40代の日本人の間では、テレビを見るよりインターネットを使っているというニュースですが、「つかみ取った」という過去の出来事を伝える動詞を現在形で表しています。過去形を使用すると、ニュースが「過去のもの」という印象になってしまいます。ニュースが古いと読者に感じさせないための工夫です。このように、多くのヘッドラインでは、ニュースの臨場感を強調するために、動詞の過去形の代わりに現在形が用いられています。

b. 未来は主に「to ＋ 動詞」で表す。

China to slow currency's fall

　中国が、自国通貨（元）の下落のスピードを押さえようとしているという、未来のことを伝えるニュースです。未来の出来事に will を使用するより、不定詞を用いた方が切れ味の良い表現となります。will があえて用いられている場合は、意志未来になることが多いです。

2 分詞の用法

a. 現在分詞は主に近い未来・予定を表す。

Vegetable prices soaring amid scorching heat

　be 動詞が、現在分詞（soaring）の前で省略されています。省略することで、語数が少なくなります。そうすることで、活字を大きくすることができ、よりヘッドラインが強調されます。また、現在分詞を用いた未来を使用すると、切迫感が強調されるという効果もあります。猛暑のため、野菜が近々高騰するという危機感が身近に感じられます。

b. 過去分詞は主に受動態を表す。

Red alerts issued for Portugal, Spain amid heat wave

　昨今、日本の夏は危険な暑さと呼ばれる熱波で苦しめられています。このヘッドラインは、be 動詞が、過去分詞 (issued) の前で省略されていますが、ポルトガルやスペインにも熱波で非常警報が発令されたというニュースです。異常気象現象は日本だけの問題ではなくなっています。

3 語数を少なくするためのさまざまな工夫

a. 冠詞・be 動詞・代名詞の所有格は省略する。

Hiroshima marks 73rd anniversary of US atomic bombing

　この例では、73rd と US の前に the が省略されています。広島が、原爆投下から 73 年目の「原爆の日」を迎えたことが伝えられています。

b. コンマにより and を省略する。

Emperor, Empress attend Hokkaido fete

　天皇・皇后両陛下が、北海道 150 年を象徴する記念式典にご出席されたというニュース報道ですが、and を省略すると畳みかけるような語調となり、メッセージが切れ味良く伝わってきます。

c. コロンにより発言者（情報源）と発言（情報）内容を分けて明示する。

State media: China won't put up with U.S. trade 'blackmail'

　米中貿易において、アメリカは中国に関税を引き上げるという「脅迫」を行いました。それに中国は耐えるつもりはないという中国政府の見解を、国営メディアが伝えています。

4 好まれる短い語

a. ピリオドによる短縮

Calif. Gov. Brown asks Trump for wildfire aid as state battles 17 blazes

　カリフォルニア州のブラウン州知事が、州内で発生した複数の山火事と闘う中、トランプ大統領に支援を求めたというニュースですが、Calif. は California、Gov. は Governor の省略です。団体や地名や人名などの固有名詞が、しばしばピリオドを用いて短縮されることがあります。

b. 頻出単語の短縮

Govt crafts aid package for flood-ravaged areas

　national や international などの頻出語は、natl や intl のように短縮されることがあります。このニュースは、政府が洪水で被災した地域に包括的な支援計画を練っていることを伝えたものですが、govt は government の短縮語です。なおこれらの短縮語は省略箇所を示すために、gov't や int'l のようにアポストロフィーを入れて表記されることもあります。

c. 略語の使用

ASEAN to back steps to denuclearize N. Korea

　東南アジア諸国連合 (ASEAN) が、北朝鮮の非核化に至る道筋において支援するつもりであるという内容の記事のヘッドラインですが、ASEAN は Association of Southeast Asian Nations の略語です。

d. 短い綴り語の使用

Minister's OK sought for Toyosu

　東京都が豊洲移転に関して農林水産大臣の認可を求めているニュース。「認可」という意味の単語には、approval や permission などがありますが、OK のように短い綴り語を使用することで、ヘッドラインの文字数削減に役立ちます。ヘッドラインは短くすればするほど、文字も大きくすることができ、メッセージを伝える威力も増します。

ヘッドラインによく用いられる短い綴り語

accord	協定	laud	賞賛する	quest	追求する
body	団体	loom	迫る	rap	非難する
boost	上げる	map	計画する	row	論争
coup	クーデター	mark	示す	rush	急ぐ
curb	抑制（する）	mart	市場	score	非難する
cut	削減（する）	nip	阻止する	slash	削除する
eye	注目する／もくろむ	nix	否認する	slay	殺す
head	率いる	nuke	核兵器	stem	阻止する
hike	引き上げる	OK	承認する	talk	会談（する）
ink	締結する	oust	追放する	term	称する
key	重要な	pact	協定	top	〜を越す
lash	攻撃する	poll	世論調査	vie	争う

5 読者を引きつける表現の工夫

For whom the Berlin Wall fell

　読者が知っている映画や本、あるいは有名人のセリフ、名言などをもじってヘッドラインが書かれることがあります。特に、意見記事やコラムのヘッドラインにこの手法がよく用いられます。このヘッドラインはアーネスト・ヘミングウェイの小説の題名 For Whom the Bell Tolls「誰がために鐘は鳴る」を明らかにもじったものです。よく知られたフレーズを用いることで、より読者の興味を引きつけるのに成功しています。「誰がためにベルリンの壁は崩壊したのか」というヘッドラインですが、ヘッドラインを見ただけで内容を読んでみたくなりますね。

B	リード

　ニュース記事の書き出しの一段落目（リード）は記事の簡潔な要約で、5Ws（Who, What, When, Where, Why）と 1H（How）の情報ができるだけ入るように書かれています。リード部分の情報は、読者が記事を先に読み進めるかどうかを決定するのに役立ち、効率的な読み方を促します。

1 ニュース記事のリード

　以下の記事は、企業提携に関する記事です。どのような情報が入っているかを確認しましょう。

Starbucks, Alibaba announce coffee delivery venture in China

　BEIJING (AP) ― Starbucks and Chinese e-commerce giant Alibaba Group announced a coffee delivery venture on Thursday, joining the growing competition in China's booming delivery industry.

(AP)

Who　　…　スターバックス社と中国の電子商取引会社アリババが
What　　…　コーヒーのデリバリー事業に乗り出すことを発表した
When　　…　木曜日に
Where　…　北京で
Why　　…　中国の運送業の競争に加わるために
How　　…　情報なし

　この記事のように、リードの前にあるニュースの発信場所を示す地名には、通信社の社名が明記されることがあります。たとえば、BEIJING (AP) は、北京から AP 通信社が発信をしているということになります。主な通信社には以下のようなものがあります。

　AP　　　　　　：Associated Press（AP 通信社）　アメリカ
　UPI　　　　　 ：United Press International（合同国際通信社）　アメリカ
　TASS　　　　　：タス通信　ロシア
　Reuters　　　 ：ロイター通信社　イギリス
　Jiji　　　　　 ：時事通信社　日本
　KYODO NEWS：共同通信社　日本
　NCNA　　　　：新華社通信社　中国
　AFP　　　　　 ：フランス通信社　フランス

2 社説・論説記事（editorial）のリード

　社説・論説記事は、一連のニュースの解説やそのニュースに対する意見を発表しています。従ってリードの部分では、当該ニュースの概要や背景がまとめられたり、ニュースに対する問題提起が行われたりします。ニュース記事と異なり、ある程度時間が経過してから書かれますので、読者がニュースについて情報を持っていることを想定し、ニュース記事のような細かい具体情報は省かれることが多いです。以下の社説のリードを見てみましょう。

Can iPS-based treatment live up to hopes of Parkinson's disease patients?
　Hope is rising among patients with Parkinson's disease, thought to number about 160,000 in Japan, following Kyoto University's latest announcement. The university should clearly ascertain the effectiveness of a new treatment utilizing induced pluripotent stem (iPS) cells.

(The Japan News)

　日本人患者数がおよそ 16 万いると思われているパーキンソン病に関して iPS 細胞を用いた新しい治療方法へ向けて新たな第一歩が踏み出されることになったと、京都大学が発表したという直前のニュース報道を受けての社説です。

　ニュース記事のリードのように、誰が、どのような治療方法を発表したのかなどの詳細な情報は掲載されず簡単にトピックの背景を紹介しているだけに留めてあります。

C ｜ ボディー

　ニュース記事と社説・論説のボディーの構造は異なります。ニュース記事は、リードで 5W1H という最重要情報が示され、その後は、より些末な具体的情報を付加していくという構造を取ります。一方、社説・論説は、リードにおいて、取り上げられたニュースの概説や問題提起、次にそのニュースに対する意見や解説、最後に結論が述べられるという構造をしています。さらに、結論部では、しばしばニュースを一般化した視点でまとめられるのも特徴です。ニュース記事のように最初に力点を置いて読むのではなく、記事全体を注意深く読む必要があります。上で取り上げた社説の最終段落では、以下のように、「iPS 細胞を臨床に応用しようという努力はいろいろな病気に対して行われてきているが、もし何かトラブルが起きたら、研究活動に支障が出るかもしれない。日本の iPS 技術は再生医療の決定的なツールなので、細心の注意を払って進めるべきである」と結論付け、医療分野への提言で締めくくられています。

Progress is being made in the effort to promote the clinical application of iPS cells in treating such illnesses as cardiac disease. If unexpected trouble cannot be properly dealt with, it could cause delays in other research activities. Japan's iPS technology can be described as its decisive tool for regenerative medicine. Extreme care should be exercised.

(*The Japan News*)

D キャプション（説明文）

　記事の写真やイラストやグラフなどの視覚情報は、記事を読む際の背景知識として非常に役立ちます。また、一種の記事の広告塔の役割を果たし、興味深い写真などが掲載されていると、記事を読む気にさせるのに役立ちます。また、写真やイラストには、キャプションと呼ばれる説明文が伴われることがあります。以下の写真のキャプションでは、子犬たちが段ボールの中に入れられ捨てられているのが写っていますが、宇都宮動物園に提供された写真であると述べられています。元の記事ではこの写真は動物園のブログに掲載されたもので、同じ飼い主による3度目の行為と推測されるとリードでは紹介されています。本文を読む際に、先に写真とキャプションに目を通しておくと、記事理解の助けになり記事を速読するのに役立ちます。

Zookeeper furious as dogs continue to be abandoned at Tochigi Pref. facility

Puppies found abandoned in a cardboard box in the Tochigi Prefecture city of Utsunomiya, on April 27, 2019, are seen in this photo provided by Utsunomiya Zoo.

(*Mainichi*)

●記事出典一覧
　（各社の承諾を得て掲載しています）

p.12　　　AP, Aug. 3, 2018

pp.13-14　The Japan News, Aug. 2, 2018

p.14　　　Mainichi, May 10, 2019

pp.17-18　The Japan News, Oct. 28, 2018

pp.21-22　The Asahi Shimbun, Jan. 5, 2019

pp.25-26　The Japan Times, Jul. 27, 2018 delivered
　　　　　by KYODO NEWS

pp.29-30　Reuters, Jul. 18, 2018

p.31　　　Rolls-Royce plc

pp.33-35　The Japan News, Jul. 24, 2018

pp.37-38　AP, Mar. 26, 2019

pp.41-42　The Asahi Shimbun, Mar. 28, 2019

pp.45-47　The Japan News, Jul. 22, 2018

pp.49-50　The Japan Times, Jan. 30, 2019

pp.53-54　The Asahi Shimbun, Jun. 26, 2018

p.55　　　MUSCA

pp.57-59　KYODO NEWS, Mar. 11, 2019

pp.61-62　The Asahi Shimbun, Jan. 27, 2019

pp.65-66　AP, Jul. 20, 2018

pp.69-71　The Asahi Shimbun, Jul. 21, 2018

pp.73-75　The Japan News, Jul. 23, 2018

●写真・図版出典一覧
　（各社の承諾を得て掲載しています）

p.16　　THE YOMIURI SHIMBUN

p.19　　井上信行／PIXTA

p.20　　The Asahi Shimbun

p.23　　菊地春香

p.24　　KYODO NEWS

p.28　　菊地春香

p.31　　Rolls-Royce plc

p.32　　THE YOMIURI SHIMBUN

p.36　　AP

p.39　　AP

p.40　　植木金矢／リイド社

p.43　　The Asahi Shimbun

p.44　　THE YOMIURI SHIMBUN

p.48　　The Japan Times

p.52　　The Asahi Shimbun

p.56　　KYODO NEWS

p.59　　iStock.com/takasuu

p.60　　The Asahi Shimbun

p.63　　The Asahi Shimbun

p.64　　Loon.

p.68　　一般社団法人佐賀県歯科医師会／
　　　　株式会社佐賀広告センター

p.71　　一般社団法人佐賀県歯科医師会／
　　　　株式会社佐賀広告センター

p.72　　THE YOMIURI SHIMBUN

chapter

1

社会・生活

お米ガチャでPR

Warm-up
1

音声を聴いて、写真を説明している英文を a 〜 c から選びましょう。

© THE YOMIURI SHIMBUN

a. ☐

b. ☐

c. ☐

Warm-up
2

現在時制は、事実、不変の真理、習慣や言葉の定義などを述べる際に用いられる時制です。日本語を参考に、音声を聴いて（　　）内に当てはまる現在時制の動詞を書き入れましょう。

1. Yamagata city（　　　　　　　　　）more young people will cook and eat rice.

山形市はもっと若い人たちにお米を炊いて食べてもらえるよう望んでいる。

2. Gacha-gacha or gachapon is a machine that usually（　　　　　　　　　）capsule toys.

ガチャガチャ、もしくはガチャポンは、通常はカプセルの入りのおもちゃを販売する機械である。

3. Autumn（　　　　　　　　　）the harvest season of rice.

秋はお米を収穫する季節である。

Warm-up 3　問 A、B に答えましょう。

 音声を聴いて、写真のコメ自販機を思いついた学生の考えとして述べられているのはどれか、1 〜 4 から選びましょう。

1．購入者にはどのブランドのお米がおいしいか知ってもらいたい。

2．購入者にはどのブランドのお米が出てくるか分からないスリルを楽しんでもらいたい。

3．若者にもっと色々なブランドのお米を味わってもらいたい。

4．若者にお米を炊く楽しさを知ってもらいたい。

Note　**Tohoku University of Art and Design**「東北芸術工科大学」

 以下の英文を読み、質問に答えましょう。

The rice vending machine was test-marketed during the campus festival earlier in October at Tohoku University of Art and Design. It has since been set up on its campus where it will remain until Nov. 3. The machine then will be set up at the university's co-op shop from Nov. 5-17. Some students are considering collecting money through crowdfunding online and plan to set up machines at michi no eki roadside rest areas in the prefecture.

(*The Japan News*)

Note　**crowdfunding**「クラウドファンディング（インターネットのサイトなどを通じて、プロジェクトなどに賛同してくれた人たちから資金を集めること）」

Which of the following statements is NOT true about the rice vending machine?

a. It was introduced experimentally at a university.

b. It is supposed to be placed on campus until Nov. 3.

c. It will be set up for about two weeks at the university's co-op store.

d. It might be placed at a railway station in the prefecture.

■ Reading

Students develop 'gacha-gacha' rice vending machine in Yamagata

YAMAGATA—A type of vending machine known as gacha-gacha or gachapon that usually dispenses capsule toys has been adapted to sell rice — an idea that began with a student of Tohoku University of Art and Design in Yamagata city who hopes more young people will cook and eat rice.

"I want more people in my generation to experience the deliciousness of Yamagata rice through gacha-gacha," said the creator of the "Yama no Okome Gacha" project, Yuika Kato, 21, a junior in the university's graphic design department.

The machine randomly discharges a pack of one of the three brands of rice harvested in Yamagata Prefecture: Haenuki, Tsuyahime or Koshihikari. Each pack contains 300 grams of rice.

Last year, Kato worked on a class assignment of "how to promote Yamagata Prefecture's charms in autumn." While brainstorming, she hit on the fact that "people around me rarely cook and eat rice. Some of them even don't have a rice cooker," she recalled.

Autumn is the harvest season of rice, and Kato launched a project with "how to make more young people eat rice grown in the prefecture" as a theme. She listed possible reasons why young people do not buy rice, based on the lifestyle environment of people in her generation. One of the problems is how people buy rice. Rice available at supermarkets usually sells per kilogram.

"Many young people don't have a car, and carrying it can be a burden," Kato said. The other problem is the portion. It is too much to eat, and some of her friends could not finish it and ended up letting it get infested by weevils. Taking the portion problem into account, she also considered a method for casually purchasing rice with a "just-for-fun attitude." And gacha-gacha, she thought, was the way.

（*The Japan News* 一部抜粋）

Notes (margin):

adapt ~「～を改変する」

discharge ~「～を出す」

work on ~「～に取り組む」
assignment「課題」
brainstorming「ブレインストーミング（あれこれ意見を検討すること）」
hit on ~「～を思いつく」

launch ~「～を開始する」

available「手に入る」

portion「分量、一人前」

end up ~ing「結局～になる」
infest「(虫が) たかる」
weevil「ゾウムシ」

■ Comprehension

Choose two statements that are true about the passage.

1. The idea of rice vending machines came from a 2nd-year university student.
2. The vending machine sells only rice grown in Yamagata.
3. Ms. Kato noticed that there were many students who cooked rice.
4. The problem was that the quantity of rice sold at supermarkets is too much and too heavy for students.
5. The reasons why young people do not buy rice were not made clear.

■ Further Activity

頭文字を参考に、以下（ガチャガチャ自販機の操作説明）の（　　）内に当てはまる適当な動詞を書き入れましょう。

© 井上信行／PIXTA

How to get a Gacha

1. Check the price mentioned on the machine.
2. （P　　　　　） the coins into the slot.
3. （T　　　　　） the tab in the direction of the arrow.
4. （G　　　　　） your capsule.

chapter

2

環境・技術

「植物の時代」の夜明け

 06

Warm-up 1

音声を聴いて、写真を説明している英文を a ～ c から選びましょう。

© The Asahi Shimbun

a. ❑

b. ❑

c. ❑

 07

Warm-up 2

1 ～ 10 は本章に登場する技術に関連する表現です。音声を聴いて、（　　）内に当てはまる語を書き入れましょう。

1. （　　　　　）substance 「木由来の物質」
2. （　　　　　）pollution 「海洋汚染」
3. （　　　　　）material 「梱包素材」
4. （　　　　　）pollution 「マイクロプラスチック汚染」
5. （　　　　　）fibers 「植物繊維」
6. （　　　　　）resin 「石油由来の樹脂」
7. （　　　　　）wood 「パウダー状の木」
8. （　　　　　）mold 「金属の鋳型」
9. （　　　　　）filing 「木の削りくず」
10. （　　　　　）resistance 「水への耐性（防水）」

Warm-up
3
問 A、B に答えましょう。

問 A　音声（Warm-up 1 の写真に写っている、プラスチックに代わる素材を研究している松岡拓磨さん〈写真右〉について）を聴いて、1 ～ 4 の中から述べられているものを選びましょう。

1．博士課程に在籍している大学院生である。

2．コンビニエンスストアの店長である。

3．店で提供しているコーヒーの材料の改良を考えている。

4．コーヒーの廃棄物の利用法の一つとしてストローを作った。

問 B　以下の英文（写真に写っている二人について）を読み、質問に答えましょう。

　　The innovative straw, which won the Japan Wood Design Award given to exceptional products or activities making use of timber, was on display at the Tokyo Big Sight exhibition center in the capital's Koto Ward Dec. 6-8. Challenges remain to be overcome for commercializing the utensil, but its inventors are looking to develop more products using their eco-friendly material.

(*The Asahi Shimbun*)

 Notes　**timber**「木材」　**utensil**「（台所用）道具」

Which of the following statements is NOT true about the two men?

a. Their product was on sale at the Tokyo Big Sight exhibition center.
b. Their product was displayed at the exhibition center for three days in a row.
c. Their wooden straw has problems to be solved before putting it on the market.
d. Their straw is made from eco-friendly material.

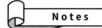

Scientists take aim at plastic with wood-based straws and more

Hiroshi Nonaka, 45, and Takuma Matsuoka, 23, developed a product in their lab at Mie University Graduate School of Bioresources using an original wood-derived substance as part of a broad vision to reduce marine pollution caused by plastics.

5 The scientists started thinking about making a straw from wood after being asked by a packing material manufacturer to replace plastic handles of paper bags with material used for paper.

In spring 2016, Nonaka began developing technology to shape a pulpy substance much like clay made from plant fibers. As plastic 10 straws have been gaining attention in relation to the problem of microplastics pollution, the researchers decided to create a wood straw as a first step.

First, powdered wood is mixed with a plant-derived substance to create the mushy material, which is then shaped with a metal mold 15 and dried. The pair refined the technique by repeatedly changing the ratio of water to thickener. The resulting straw, which has a 5-mm inside diameter, is free of oil-based resin or adhesive materials.

While making straws from wood by simply cutting and shaving timber would lead to a large amount of wood filings, the newly 20 developed technology can be used to create wooden straws without producing such waste. "Our straws can be made even from sawdust, and the substance can be shaped freely," Nonaka said.

Nonaka and Matsuoka plan to use their wood-derived material to replace not only plastic straws, but also plastic trays and shampoo 25 bottles. However, there are still hurdles to overcome before commercial operations can start. When soaked in water for an extended period, the thickener starts dissolving and the straw swells up. It can also become deformed during the drying process. For these reasons, it is difficult to mass produce the straw at this point. "The 30 next challenge is how to improve the straw's water resistance and enable it to maintain its shape," said Nonaka.

(*The Asahi Shimbun* 一部抜粋)

---

bioresouce「生物資源」

shape ～「～を成形する」
pulpy「パルプ状の」
clay「粘土」

mushy「粥状の」
refine ～「～を改良する」
thickener「増粘剤」
adhesive material「接着剤」

sawdust「おがくず」

replace ～「～の代わりとなる」

dissolve「溶ける」
swell up「膨らむ」
deform「変形する」

■ Comprehension

Choose two statements that are true about the passage.

1. The researchers' main purpose for developing the wood straw is to maintain forest resources.
2. They were asked to develop a packing material to replace paper bags.
3. Mushy material is created by mixing a plant-derived substance and powdered wood.
4. Their technology can make straws from wood by simply cutting and shaving timber.
5. It is difficult to produce their wood straw on a large scale now.

■ Further Activity

以下はあるハワイアンカフェの宣伝からの抜粋です。このカフェで使用されているストローの代用品の食品は何か考えてみましょう。（　　）内に最初の文字と文字数がヒントで与えられています。

"One straw at a time" is a serious global problem. We have come up with an idea to solve this problem. When used, it will become a little sticky, but there is no real problem downing the drink. Enjoy tropical drinks with our original, fanciful straw made of hard (p＿ ＿ ＿ ＿)！

国際

緊急速報も国際化

11

Warm-up
1

音声を聴いて、写真を説明している英文を a ～ c から選びましょう。

© KYODO NEWS

a. ☐

b. ☐

c. ☐

12

Warm-up
2

名詞を形容する表現は、単独の形容詞の場合は前に、複数の単語で修飾する場合は後ろに置かれます。音声を聴いて、下線部の名詞を修飾している表現を完成させましょう。

1. people on (＿＿＿＿＿＿＿＿)　　　乗客たち

2. a (＿＿＿＿＿＿) man (＿＿＿＿＿＿＿) (＿＿＿＿＿＿＿) helplessly

　　　　　　　　　　　　　　　　　　途方に暮れて立っている外国人の男性

3. (＿＿＿＿＿＿＿) service　　　中断されたサービス

4. a (＿＿＿＿＿) staff in (＿＿＿＿＿) of assisting people in a crisis

　　　　　　　　　　　　　　　　　　危機の時に人々を助ける担当の日本人スタッフ

5. a (＿＿＿＿＿＿) member (＿＿＿＿＿) (＿＿＿＿＿＿) her the microphone　　　彼女にマイクを渡した乗務員

3

問 A、B に答えましょう。

問 A

音声を聴いて、大阪府で起きた強い地震について、1 ～ 4 の中から<u>述べられていないもの</u>を選びましょう。

1．地震が起こったのは先月であった。

2．地震は 6 月 18 日の午前 8 時ごろに起きた。

3．地震速報のアラームが鳴り、駅員が乗客に降りるよう指示した。

4．その電車は芦屋駅で停止した。

問 B

以下の英文を読み、本文の内容に合うように英文を完成しましょう。

Tobu Railway Co., whose network covers the Kanto region including Tokyo and the four surrounding prefectures, started an emergency announcement system using four languages — Japanese, English, Chinese and Korean — at nine stations frequented by visitors, including Asakusa and Tokyo Skytree stations.

Tablet computers are installed at the stations to provide announcements in the four languages in the event of accidents and disasters.

(*The Japan Times delivered by KYODO NEWS*)

Which of the following statements is true about the passage?

a. People can get emergency alerts in Japanese and two other languages.

b. Asakusa is one of visitors' favorite destinations.

c. Every station of Tobu Railway Co. has tablet computers for alert announcements.

d. The tablet computers installed at the stations can be used anytime.

■ Reading

Calls for multilingual alert systems grow in Japan as visitors crowd mass transport

As the continuing tourism boom packs public transportation systems nationwide, developing multilingual emergency alerts is becoming a top priority.

In public transport emergencies, there are often no emergency
5 announcements in English or other languages, leaving both foreign passengers and the Japanese staff in charge of assisting them in a crisis.

At around 8 a.m. on June 18, alarms from the earthquake early warning system went off, prompting the train to slow down before coming to a halt at Ashiya Station in Hyogo Prefecture. Hikaru
10 Nagano, 52, a Kobe resident who works for a broadcasting station in the city of Osaka, noticed a foreign man standing around helplessly with no clue about what was happening and explained to him in English that the train had stopped due to an earthquake. The man was from India.

15 Nagano, who has worked abroad on several occasions, thought there might be more foreign people on board struggling to figure out what was happening. So she rushed to the driver's compartment and volunteered to make an emergency announcement in English. Although surprised by the suggestion, a crew member handed her the
20 microphone.

"This is an emergency announcement. There was a strong earthquake in Osaka," Nagano said, adding that the train would be held at the station for a while. Once service was suspended, she directed passengers in English to the exits.

25 While relieved to see so many foreign riders exit without problems, she was also concerned that she might have overstepped her authority.

(*The Japan Times delivered by KYODO NEWS* 一部抜粋)

multilingual「多言語の」

mass transport「大量輸送機関」

priority「最優先課題」

in a crisis「危険にさらされている」

prompt ... to ~「…に~するよう促す」
halt「停止」

clue「手がかり」

figure out ~「~を理解する」

volunteer to ~「~することを申し出る」

overstep ~「~を踏み越える」
authority「職権」

■ Comprehension

Choose two statements that are true about the passage.

1. Railway companies have already developed multilingual alert systems.
2. Emergency announcements are often made both in Japanese and English.
3. A man from India had no idea about what was happening when the earthquake occurred.
4. Ms. Nagano asked the driver to make an emergency announcement in English.
5. She was relieved to see many passengers get off the train safely.

■ Further Activity

以下のスマートフォンの緊急地震速報の画面に<u>述べられていない</u>情報を選択肢からすべて選びましょう。

Safety tips
Earthquake Early Warning (EEW)
Intensity : 5 Lower
Coming : after 10 seconds
Occurred at : 2017/03/14 20:20:20
Epicenter : Naka-dori District, Fukushima Pref
Max Intensity : 5 Lower
Close View

a. 震度 　　　b. 発生時間 　　　c. 震源地

d. 震源の深さ 　　e. 避難勧告

chapter

4 経済・科学技術 アストンマーティン空を飛ぶ

16 | **Warm-up 1**

音声を聴いて、イラスト（アストンマーティン社が発表した車のコンセプトデザイン）を説明している英文を a〜c から選びましょう。

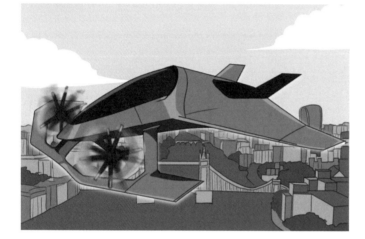

a. ❏

b. ❏

c. ❏

17 | **Warm-up 2**

現在完了「have/has ＋過去分詞 (Ved)」という時制は、過去と現在の関わりを説明する表現で、「過去から現在まである動作・状態が続いていること」または「その動作・状態が現在までに終わってしまっていること」などを表しています。音声を聴いて、1〜3 の英文を完成しましょう。

1. Aston Martin（　　　　　　　　　　）up with a futuristic personal flying aircraft.
「アストンマーティン社は、未来の空飛ぶ自家用車を思いついた」
　　→過去に思いついただけでなく、現在それを実現しようとしている

2. Aston Martin（　　　　　　　　　　）with a variety of organizations.
「アストンマーティン社は、様々な団体と提携している」
　　→過去に提携し、現在もその関係が続いている

3. Some companies（　　　　　　　　　　）plans for a flying taxi.
「空飛ぶタクシーの計画を発表した企業もある」
　　→過去に計画を発表し、現在もその計画が続いている。

音声（前ページのイラストのコンセプトデザインについて）を聴いて、<u>述べられていないもの</u>を選びましょう。

1. このコンセプトデザインを発表したのは、アストンマーティン社の副社長である。

2. コンセプトデザインによると、垂直離着陸機能を装備している。

3. コンセプトデザインによると、毎時200キロメートル飛行が可能である。

4. この車なら、バーミンガムの市街地からロンドンの市街地まで約30分で行ける。

以下の英文を読み、本文の内容に合うように英文を完成しましょう。

Commenting on how to pilot the vehicle, Helen Atkinson, a professor at Cranfield University, said: "You've got to detect what's going on in the external environment and then turn that around incredibly quickly in the computer system with the artificial intelligence built in to actually achieve the necessary level of autonomy."

(*Reuters*)

Notes detect ~「～を検知する」　autonomy「自律性」

According to Professor Helen Atkinson,

a. the pilot of the car has to turn the car around to see the external environment.
b. she herself does not know how to pilot the car.
c. the pilot of the car cannot detect what happens outside the car.
d. the car is to be equipped with an automatic operating system.

■ Reading

Aston Martin unveils 'sports car for the skies' at airshow

FARNBOROUGH, England (Reuters) - James Bond would love it. Aston Martin, maker of the luxury sports cars favored by the fictional British spy, has come up with a futuristic personal aircraft it has dubbed "a sports car for the skies."

5   Aston Martin unveiled the three-seater hybrid-electric vehicle this week at the Farnborough Airshow and, though the concept remains for now the stuff of science fiction, believes it could help one day to revolutionize travel.

Aviation and technology leaders are working to make electric-
10 powered flying taxis a reality, including Airbus, U.S. ride-sharing firm Uber and a range of start-ups including one backed by Google co-founder Larry Page, called Kitty Hawk.

Aston Martin believes it could corner the market for luxury flying vehicles in the future.

15 "The same way that you have Uber and you have an Aston Martin, you'll have 'Uber in the skies' and you'll have 'Aston Martin in the skies,'" said Simon Sproule, vice president of Aston Martin, adding that such an aircraft won't come cheap.

"This is clearly a luxury object ─ it's a sports car for the skies ─
20 so pricing is going to be commensurate with that, so certainly into the seven figures."

The company has partnered with Cranfield University, Cranfield Aerospace Solutions and British jet engine maker Rolls-Royce to develop the concept vehicle, including artificial intelligence-powered
25 autonomous capabilities.

"It feels like a fighter jet but at the same time it has the Aston Martin luxury," said David Debney, chief of future aircraft concepts at Rolls-Royce.

(*Reuters* 一部抜粋)

favor ~ 「～を好む」
fictional 「架空の」
come up with ~ 「～を思いつく」
dub ~ 「～と呼ぶ」

for now 「現在のところ」

aviation 「航空学」

start-up 「新興企業」

corner the market 「市場を支配する」

pricing 「価格設定」
commensurate with ~ 「～に見合う」

capability 「機能」

■ Comprehension

Choose two statements that are true about the passage.

1. James Bond is a maker of the luxury sports car.
2. The concept car of Aston Martin was sold at the Farnborough Airshow.
3. Aston Martin believes it could dominate the market for flying cars.
4. Some companies want to push through electric-powered flying taxis.
5. The flying cars will come cheap thanks to their mass production.

■ Further Activity

以下（ロールスロイス社の HP の press release）を読んで、コンセプトデザインが応用できる用途として、述べられていないものを 1 ～ 5 から選びましょう。

© Rolls-Royce plc

The Rolls-Royce EVTOL project

Rolls-Royce has unveiled a concept electric vertical take-off and landing (EVTOL) vehicle at the Farnborough International Airshow 2018. The design could be adapted for personal transport, public transport, logistics and military applications and is based upon technologies that already exist or are currently under development. It could take to the skies as soon as the early 2020s.

https://www.rolls-royce.com/media/our-stories/discover/2018/ blue-sky-thinking-rr-unveils-evtol-concept-at-farnborough-airshow.aspx

1. 自家用　　2. 軍用　　　3. 公共輸送用
4. 物流用　　5. 宇宙旅行用

chapter 5

環境・科学技術

5 AIが「想定外」をなくす お手伝い

21

Warm-up 1

音声を聴いて、イラストのシステム（衛星と地上の情報を使った災害予測システム）の説明をしている英文を a ～ c から選びましょう。

Disaster prediction system using data from satellites, land

Satellite data (location information, observation)

AI analysis

Ground, water level changes

Analysis, prediction through AI

Land-based data (meteorological information)

Detect signs of landslides, sinking of roads

Call for caution, evacuations

© THE YOMIURI SHIMBUN

a. ❏

b. ❏

c. ❏

22

Warm-up 2

"and" という接続詞は、前後にくる単語によって発音が変化します。and が子音で終わる語に続いたり、and が母音で始まる語の前にきたりすると音がつながります。また、子音で始まる語が後ろに続く場合に、/d/ 音がはっきり聞こえないこと（以下 ɗ と表記）があります。音声を聴いて（　　）内に当てはまる適当な単語を書き入れましょう。

1. data from both (　　　　　　　) and (　　　　　　　) ground
   「衛星と地上からのデータ」

2. changes in terrain, (　　　　　　　) and (　　　　　　　) factors
   「地形や降雨やその他の要因の変化」

3. issue (　　　　　　　) and (　　　　　　　) orders
   「警報や避難指示を発令する」

4. observe the amount of (　　　　　　　) and (　　　　　　　) condition
   of the terrain
   「雨量と地形の状態を観察する」

Warm-up **3** 問 A、B に答えましょう。

 問 A 音声を聴いて、1～4の中から述べられているものを選びましょう。

1．災害時は、政府や地方自治体の迅速な判断が重要である。

2．想定外の災害に備える警報システムの整備が急がれる。

3．政府や地方自治体は、災害予測の精度を上げる方法を検討する必要がある。

4．政府は、地方自治体に正確な災害予測を行うように指示している。

 問 B 以下の英文（前ページのイラストに示された災害予測の新システムについて）、質問に答えましょう。

Under the new system, disaster-prone locations will be designated in advance as monitoring spots, based on relevant information including hazard maps developed by local governments. Sensors will be placed at these locations to observe the amount of rainfall and the condition of the terrain.

(*The Japan News*)

 Notes **disaster-prone**「災害を受けやすい」 **designate**「指定する」

Which of the following information is NOT used for the new system?

a. Maps that highlight areas that are affected by disasters
b. Changes in the amount of precipitation
c. Changes in the vertical and horizontal dimensions of land surface
d. The number of designated monitoring spots

New satellite-based system eyed for disaster prediction

The government plans to launch a new disaster prediction system in fiscal 2020, using data from both satellites and the ground, in an effort to enable local governments to efficiently call for quick evacuations in the event of signs of a natural disaster.

5 Using artificial intelligence, the system will analyze data round the clock — checking changes in terrain, rainfall and other factors — from monitoring spots where such disasters as landslides and floods are likely to occur.

The system was proposed at a July 4 meeting of the Internal 10 Affairs and Communications Ministry's panel of experts, which is tasked with discussing how to further harness satellite data, and led by Prof. Shinichi Nakasuka of the University of Tokyo.

Following the proposal, the ministry has appropriated necessary funds through its budgetary request for fiscal 2019 to realize 15 the system in cooperation with such authorities as the Land, Infrastructure, Transport and Tourism Ministry and the Japan Meteorological Agency.

Under the new system, the Michibiki quasi-zenith satellite system (see below) will be used to get relevant data — on about an hourly 20 basis — such as changes in terrain, rainfall and soil saturation. In addition, the data and other meteorological information will be examined using artificial intelligence software to gauge the disaster risk.

The new system is expected to accurately forecast the locations 25 of disasters, which enables local governments to effectively issue warnings and evacuation orders to residents.

(*The Japan News* 一部抜粋)

*the Internal Affairs and Communications Ministry「総務省」
*the Land, Infrastructure, Transport and Tourism Ministry「国土交通省」
*the Japan Meteorological Agency「気象庁」

eye ~「〜を計画する」

launch ~「〜を開始する」
in an effort to ~「〜する目的で」

in the event of ~「〜のときに」

panel of experts「有識者会議」
be tasked with ~「〜が任務の」
harness ~「〜を活用する」

appropriate funds「資金を計上する」
budgetary「予算の」

authority「官庁」

hourly「毎時の」

soil saturation「土壌浸透」

meteorological「気象の」

gauge ~「〜を正しく判断する」

■ Comprehension

Choose two statements that are true about the passage.

1. Local governments need to issue quick evacuation orders at the time of disasters.
2. The system will analyze data day and night using artificial intelligence.
3. Monitoring spots are the places where disasters have already occurred.
4. Artificial intelligence does not analyze meteorological information.
5. According to a ministry official, the system is not useful for disaster-prone locations.

■ Further Activity

新聞記事では、記事の付加情報が最後に添えられることがあります。本文に入れ込むと記事の流れが阻害されるからです。前ページの記事中の(see below)は「以下参照」という意味で、「記事の最後を参照せよ」という指示です。

以下は、前ページの記事末に、三菱電機の準天頂衛星システムについての付加情報として加えられていたものです。英文の内容に合うものを、1～4から選びましょう。

■ **Quasi-zenith satellite system :** A Japanese positioning satellite system that transmits radio waves from space and provides location information on objects on the ground

   The satellites travel over Japan in a quasi-zenith orbit, thereby preventing signal blockage by mountains or high-rise structures. The satellites are expected to provide highly accurate measurements with a margin of error of about several centimeters. A total of four satellites have been launched to provide positioning information from November of this year.

(The Japan News)

---

1. 衛星は、地上にある山や高層ビルから発信される電波を観測する。
2. 衛星は、日本の上空の準天頂軌道を周回している。
3. 測定値の誤差は全くなく、非常に正確な位置情報を提供する。
4. 今年11月までに、全部で4機の衛星が打ち上げられる予定である。

chapter 6

環境・医療

野生動物を救え！

26 Warm-up **1**
音声を聴いて、写真（南アフリカ共和国の都市ヨハネスブルグにある野生動物の病院）に写っているスタッフを説明している英文を a 〜 c から選びましょう。

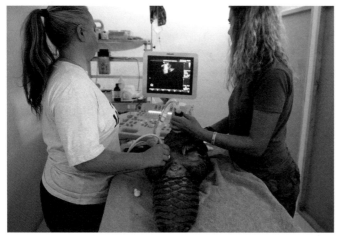

© AP

a. ☐

b. ☐

c. ☐

27 Warm-up **2**
1 〜 5 の下線部に適当な文字を書き入れて単語を完成し、（　　）内に適当な前置詞を書き入れ、音声を聴いて解答を確認しましょう。

1. Wild animals i＿＿＿＿＿（　　　　　　）the region
「その地域土着の野生動物」

2. be s＿＿＿＿＿ out（　　　　　　）the rapid urbanization
「急速な都市化によって追いやられる」

3. d＿＿＿＿＿ an animal（　　　　　）a pet
「動物をペットとして飼い慣らす」

4. b＿＿＿＿＿ electric light（　　　　　）disturbing the animals
「動物たちを怯えさせないように電気の光を遮る」

5. s＿＿＿＿＿（　　　　　　）trauma　「トラウマに苦しむ」

Warm-up

3　問 A、B に答えましょう。

28 　問 **A**　音声を聴いて、ヨハネスブルグの野生動物の病院について述べられているものはどれか、1 ～ 4 から選びましょう。

1．この病院には約 60 匹の動物が入院している。

2．入院しているヒョウモンガメは 6 匹である。

3．12 フィートのパイソンは 2 匹いる。

4．カワウソは病院でペットとして育てられている。

 Notes　leopard tortoise「ヒョウモンガメ」　toothless「歯の抜けた」　python「パイソン（蛇の一種）」
otter「カワウソ」

29 　問 **B**　以下の英文を読み、質問に答えましょう。

Along with five staffers, the veterinary hospital relies on volunteers like Lauren Beckley, who lives nearby. Beckley cares for young primates like baboons and vervet monkeys, who cling to her after their own mothers have been shot or run over by humans.

Other wildlife at the hospital include two newly born bush babies which are small nocturnal primates. One has been attacked by a cat and the other has fallen out of its nest.

(AP)

Notes　veterinary hospital「動物病院」　primate「霊長類」　baboon「ヒヒ」　vervet monkey「ベルベットモンキー」
wildlife「野生動物」　bush baby「ガラゴ」　nocturnal「夜行性の」

Which of the following statements is true about the passage?

a. The wildlife hospital has six staff who take care of the animals.

b. Beckley tries to prevent animals from getting hurt by people.

c. Other wildlife hospitals also help animals return to the wild.

d. One of the two newly born bush babies has been injured from falling from their nest.

■ Reading

Johannesburg wildlife clinic saves animals hurt in city

JOHANNESBURG (AP) — At the edge of sprawling Johannesburg suburbs, a veterinary hospital is saving the lives of wildlife on the urban fringes.

"I'd love to be in the bush, but I get more cases here," said
5 veterinary rehabilitation specialist Nicci Wright.

Wright founded the hospital two years ago with veterinarian Dr. Karin Lourens and since then has treated about 4,000 animals.

With the expansion of Pretoria and Johannesburg, South Africa's capital city and its economic center, the animals indigenous to the
10 region are being squeezed out by the rapid urbanization. The wildlife hospital mainly treats small mammals and raptors that are injured.

There are about 160 animals on the small premises now, including half a dozen leopard tortoises, a toothless 12-foot python and an otter that was taken far from her natural habitat when someone tried to
15 domesticate her as a pet.

A Johannesburg resident arrives at the hospital, carrying a gray lourie in a cage made for a much smaller domesticated bird. He found the large bird in the garden, attacked by his dogs, unable to fly after its tail and wing feathers were plucked out. Like in any hospital, nurse
20 Alicia Abbott opens a file and transfers the new patient to a more comfortable setting so its treatment may begin.

Most of the cages in the hospital are covered with towels to block the electric light from disturbing the animals. Along with physical injuries, many of them also suffer from trauma. Some species, like
25 the endangered pangolin, show visible signs of post-traumatic stress disorder when they hear a male human voice or smell cigarette smoke, a reminder of the poachers who hunt them, said Wright.

(AP 一部抜粋)

sprawling「広大な」

suburbs「郊外」

on the urban fringes「都会の周辺に」
in the bush「奥地に」
veterinary rehabilitation「動物医療リハビリテーション」
veterinarian「獣医」

expansion「発展」

mammal「哺乳動物」
raptor「猛禽類」
premise「敷地」

habitat「生息地」

resident「住民」
gray lourie「ムジハイイロエボシドリ」
domesticated bird「家禽」

pluck out ~「~を引き抜く」

endangered「絶滅の危機にある」
pangolin「センザンコウ」
post-traumatic stress disorder「心的外傷後ストレス障害」
reminder「存在を思い出させるもの」
poacher「密猟者」

■ Comprehension

Choose two statements that are true about the passage.

1. This hospital in Johannesburg is trying to save wildlife.
2. They have treated many animals at this hospital since several years ago.
3. They treat only small mammals and raptors.
4. Alicia Abbott works as a nurse in this hospital.
5. A few of the animals in the hospital suffer from trauma.

■ Further Activity

以下は、本文の記事に付けられている写真です。この写真に最も適当と思われるキャプション（写真の解説文）をa～cから選びましょう。

© AP

a. With the expansion of urban areas, the animals indigenous to the region are being squeezed out by development.
b. The wildlife hospital mainly treats small mammals and raptors that are injured.
c. A sick bird is being protected at the veterinary hospital.

7

社会・労働

人生 100 年、どう生きる?

 31

Warm-up
1

音声(植木金矢氏の漫画について)を聴いて、イラストを説明している英文を a 〜 c から選びましょう。

© 植木金矢／リイド社

a. ☐

b. ☐

c. ☐

32

Warm-up
2

1 〜 8 の下線部に適当な文字を書き入れて単語を完成し、(　　)内に適当な前置詞を書き入れ、音声を聴いて解答を確認しましょう。

1. make a n＿＿＿＿＿(　　　　　　) oneself 「名をあげる」

2. make a c＿＿＿＿＿ 「復帰する」

3. retire (　　　　　)a commercial manga creator 「商業漫画家として退職する」

4. retire (　　　　) c＿＿＿＿＿ manga 「漫画を描くことを辞める」

5. climb the stairs (　　　　) both h＿＿＿＿＿ and l＿＿＿＿＿
「四つん這いで階段を上る」

6. compare 〜 (　　　　　) … 「〜と…を比較する」

7. hit (　　　　) new stories 「新しいストーリーを思いつく」

8. emerge (　　　　) s＿＿＿＿＿ 「次々と現れる」

問 A、B に答えましょう。

問
A

音声（年齢と絵を描く技術の関係について）を聴いて、述べられているのはどれか、
1〜4 から選びましょう。

1．葛飾北斎は 89 歳で亡くなる時まで現役の画家だった。

2．彼の絵を描く技術は高齢になると衰えた。

3．彼は高齢になるほど観察力は伸びると主張した。

4．彼は年齢に応じた絵の技術の伸ばし方を後世に伝えた。

問
B

以下の英文（植木金矢氏の経歴について）を読み、質問に答えましょう。

　　Born in 1921 — earlier than Osamu Tezuka, who is known as "the god of manga," and Shigeru Mizuki, who continued aggressively creating manga just before his death — Ueki decided to be a painter after reading "Norakuro" by Suiho Tagawa during his childhood. As his father strongly opposed his plan, Ueki joined the Japanese military and fought in China during World War II. Following the end of the war, he asked publishing firms to allow him to illustrate magazines while working at a factory.

(*The Asahi Shimbun*)

Notes **aggressively**「精力的に」　**oppose ~**「〜に反対する」

Which of the following statements is true about the passage?

a．Osamu Tezuka and Shigeru Mizuki were born in the same year.

b．Ueki was inspired by a manga artist and started to read Tagawa's manga.

c．He gave up his dream because World War II began.

d．After the war ended, he worked as a factory worker.

■ Reading

Active 97-year-old manga artist inspires younger creators

Kinya Ueki, 97, who made a name for himself in boys' comics and pioneered the "gekiga" (dramatic pictures) manga genre, once retired as a commercial manga creator but made a comeback after turning 80.

Even after passing the 90-year milestone, Ueki remained active, 5 including releasing a 200-page comic book late last year.

On a recent day, Ueki was seen climbing the stairs with both hands and legs to the second floor of his home, where he writes and illustrates his works without the help of assistants.

As his eyesight has weakened and his hands have become shaky 10 since he turned 90, it is difficult for Ueki to draw straight lines or paint detailed pictures. Comparing his works with manga by younger artists in the same magazine, Ueki finds his style outdated.

As for why he does not retire from creating manga, Ueki cited his "never-give-up spirit." "It is natural for such an elderly man to 15 become unable to paint as I want to do. But I hit upon new stories, so I want to continue working for as long as I can," he said.

His manga featuring sword fighting, such as "Fuun Kurama Hicho" and "Mikazuki Tengu," proved popular among boys' comic readers, when he was around 30. Ueki released works in many magazines in 20 the 1950s to 1960s.

Since Ueki originally wanted to be a painter, he did not know much about manga, so he created manga based on his beloved film "Kurama Tengu." His realistic illustrations and film-like stories inspired by the movie captured the hearts of young readers.

25 "At the time, parents did not want their children to read manga," Ueki said. "New manga artists emerged in succession. When I read a manga of Fujio Akatsuka for the first time, I was surprised that artists with new talents like him appeared."

(*The Asahi Shimbun* 一部抜粋)

Notes

inspire ~「~を鼓舞する」

pioneer ~「~の先駆者となる」

milestone「一里塚」
release ~「~を発表する」

outdated「時代遅れの」

as for ~「~に関しては」
cite ~「~を引用する」

feature ~「~を特徴とする」
sword fighting「チャンバラ」
prove ~「~であることが分かる」

beloved「大好きな」

realistic「写実的な」

■ Comprehension

Choose two statements that are true about the passage.

1. Mr. Ueki used to be a commercial manga artist.
2. When he was 80, he retired from work.
3. He thinks his manga style is as new as younger manga artists'.
4. His motto is "never give up."
5. He became popular among readers 30 years ago.

■ Further Activity

以下のキャプション（写真を説明する文）の（　　）内に当てはまる適当な語を、本文の中から探し、必要なら形を変えて書き入れましょう。

© The Asahi Shimbun

Kinya Ueki（　　　　　　　）manga in his workroom lined with video and cassette tapes on the（　　　　　　　）（　　　　　　　）of his home.

8

国際・医療

救急医療にレスキュー

Warm-up 1 音声を聴いて、イラストを説明している英文を a 〜 c から選びましょう。

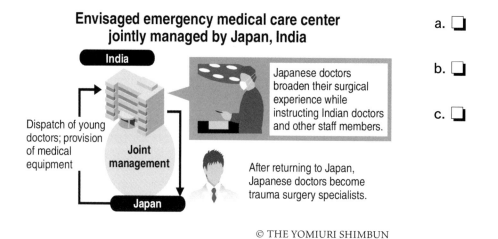

Envisaged emergency medical care center jointly managed by Japan, India

India

Dispatch of young doctors; provision of medical equipment

Joint management

Japan

Japanese doctors broaden their surgical experience while instructing Indian doctors and other staff members.

After returning to Japan, Japanese doctors become trauma surgery specialists.

a. ☐

b. ☐

c. ☐

© THE YOMIURI SHIMBUN

Warm-up 2 意味のつながりが強い2つの単語の連なりにおいて、子音で終わる語の次に母音で始まる語がくると音がつながって聞こえます。以下の音声を聴いて、( ) 内に適当な単語を書き入れましょう。

1. an ( ) medical care center ( ) in trauma surgery

 「外傷外科手術が専門の救命救急センター」

2. an ( ) for Japanese doctors to perform trauma surgeries

 「日本人医師が外傷外科手術をする機会」

3. accumulate ( ) for ( ) certain period at designated special facilities

 「指定の専門施設で一定期間の経験を積む」

Warm-up 3

問 A、B に答えましょう。

問 A

音声（前ページのイラストの救命救急センターが設立されることになった、インド国内の背景について）を聴いて、以下の文中の空所に適当な数字を書き入れましょう。

インド政府によると、同国で（**1.** 　　　　　）年の交通事故死者数が（**2.** 　　　　　）人を越え、世界（**3.** 　　　　）位になったことから、その対策を講じるのが緊急の課題となっている。

問 B

以下の英文（インドに救命救急センターを設立することになった、日本とインド両国の国内事情について）を読み、質問に答えましょう。

　　Use of motor vehicles is rapidly increasing in India, but so is the number of traffic accidents as infrastructure improvement has not kept pace with the growth in motor vehicle use.

　　Meanwhile in Japan, the number of traffic accidents is on the decline. The opportunities for emergency trauma surgical operations have decreased [in Japan], and now it is difficult to train Japanese doctors who specialize in trauma surgery here.

(*The Japan News*)

 Notes keep pace with ~「～についていく」　meanwhile「一方」　emergency trauma surgical operation「外傷緊急手術」

Why do the Japanese and Indian governments plan to jointly build an emergency medical care center in India?

a. Because of the increase in traffic accidents in India

b. Because of the creation of infrastructure in India

c. Because of the increase in traffic accidents in Japan

d. Because of the shortage of medical doctors in Japan

Japan, India to train trauma surgeons

The Japanese and Indian governments plan to jointly build an emergency medical care center specializing in trauma surgery in the Indian capital city of New Delhi in response to mounting demand for trauma surgery mainly due to a rapid increase in traffic accidents in
5 India.

The Japanese government intends to dispatch young doctors to India and contribute to nurturing Indian doctors, and at the same time, it wants to make the medical exchange with India an opportunity for Japanese doctors to broaden their surgical experience, according to
10 sources.

The initiative is aimed at promotion of Japan's medical and nursing care service industries through overseas deployment. And at the same time the government intends to help Asian countries build societies that can cope with aging populations.

15 The center will be housed in the All India Institute of Medical Sciences, which is regarded as the best medical university in the country. The activities at the center will include Japanese doctors teaching Indian participants how to use state-of-the-art medical equipment introduced from Japan.

20 The Japanese government expects that young Japanese doctors dispatched to India will broaden their experience with emergency trauma surgeries at the center, and the center will become an opportunity to nurture the Japanese specialist doctors.

In order to be certified in Japan as a special doctor for trauma
25 surgery, it is necessary to accumulate experience for a certain period at designated special facilities. The Japanese government plans to urge the domestic medical groups to take into consideration the records of operations in India in the screening process to certify the specialist doctors.

(*The Japan News* 一部抜粋)

in response to ~「〜に対応して」
mount「高まる」

dispatch ~「〜を派遣する」

nurture ~「〜を育成する」

surgical「外科手術の」

sources「消息筋」

initiative「新たな取り組み」
promotion「振興」
deployment「展開」

cope with ~「〜対処する」

house in ~「〜内に設置する」

state-of-the-art「最新の」

certify ... as ~「…を〜に認定する」

screening「審査の」

■ Comprehension

Choose two statements that are true about the passage.

1. Demand for trauma surgery is increasing in Japan.
2. The Japanese government will send young Japanese doctors to India to train Indian doctors.
3. The joint project between Japan and India intends to promote Japan's medical industry.
4. Most of the Indian doctors specialize in emergency trauma surgeries.
5. The records of operations in India are essential to be certified as a traumatologist in Japan.

■ Further Activity

以下の表は、今後の日本とインド両政府の取り組みについてまとめたものです。表を説明する英文中に、当てはまる語を選択肢から選んで書き入れましょう。

	取り組み内容
日本政府	・「健康・医療戦略推進本部」の会議を開催予定 ・「健康・医療戦略推進本部」の会議において「アジア健康構想」の基本方針を改定する予定 ・救命救急センターの設立を「アジア健康構想」の基本方針に盛り込む
インド政府	・救命救急センターの設立を目指す

　　The Japanese government is considering （**1.**　　　　） a meeting of its Headquarters for Healthcare Policy to （**2.**　　　　） the basic policy of the Asia Human Well-Being Initiative to （**3.**　　　　） the establishment of the emergency medical care center in the policy. The Indian side is （**4.**　　　　） to open an emergency medical care center in cooperation with the Japanese government.

(*The Japan News*)

include	revise	aiming	holding

chapter

9

国際・経済

なぜ今「グローバル化」？

 41

Warm-up 1

以下は、あるイベントに出席している楽天の CEO 三木谷浩史氏（右）とハーバードビジネススクールの教授トセダール・ニーリー氏（左）の写真です。音声を聴いて、写真を説明している英文を a ～ c から選びましょう。

a. ❏

b. ❏

c. ❏

© The Japan Times

 42

Warm-up 2

ある単語の終わりの子音と、続く単語の初めの子音が同じ場合にも、前章で学習した音がつながる現象がおこります。音声を聴いて 1 ～ 5 の（　）内に当てはまる語句を書き取りましょう。さらに、書き取った語句について音がつながって聞こえる部分に下線を引きましょう。

1.　（ 　　　　　　　　　3 語) the demand　「需要についていく」

2.　be coupled with rising demand for (　　　　　　　 2 語)

　　「腕のある開発者の高まる需要と相まっている」

3.　be (　　　　　　　　　3 語) software programming skills

　　「ソフトウェアのプログラム技能を必要としている」

4.　hire (　　　　　　　　 2 語) in large numbers　「大量に外国人エンジニアを雇う」

5.　（ 　　　　　　　　　3 語) the core of a company's business

　　「会社の事業の中核に関与する」

問 A、B に答えましょう。

問 A　音声を聴いて、最近の多くの日本の新興企業の傾向として述べられているのはどれか、1～4から選びましょう。

1. 徐々に職場に外国人を登用していっている。

2. 企業開設当初から外国人を登用している。

3. グローバル化に備えて、職場で複数の言語を使用するようにしている。

4. グローバル化に備えて、職場で複数の言語を話せる日本人を採用している。

問 B　以下の英文（様々な難点があるにも関わらず外国人エンジニアが日本で働きたいと述べていることついて）を読み、質問に答えましょう。

　　Japanese companies' slow decision-making can feel particularly frustrating in a field that is supposed to be fast-moving. Compensation levels for programmers in Japan tend to be much lower than in other countries, and particularly low in comparison with Silicon Valley standards. However, many non-Japanese software engineers have said they were happy to trade lower compensation for the chance to live and work here in Japan.

(*The Japan Times*)

Notes decision-making「意志決定」 compensation「報酬」

Which of the following statements is true about in the passage?

a. Frustration caused by the fast-moving IT industry

b. A characteristic of Japanese companies

c. Minimum wage paid to workers from other countries

d. Programming skills of engineers in Silicon Valley

■ Reading

Demand for non-Japanese engineers is growing

IT engineering is a field in which there are a lot of opportunities for non-Japanese who possess sufficient skills to work in Japan. There are 28,000 non-Japanese IT engineers working in Japan currently, comprising about 3 percent of all IT engineers in Japan, according to
5 the Ministry of Economy, Trade and Industry. The ministry projects that Japan will face a deficit of 789,000 software engineers by 2030, a gap that non-Japanese engineers are well-positioned to help fill.

The reason behind the need for engineers is in part the same as in other fields: the aging population here means there are fewer working-
10 age people. Also, Japanese universities can't produce enough software engineers to keep up with the demand, especially in fields such as databases and AI development. This is coupled with rising demand for skilled software developers, due to increase of software-based technologies such as AI, web-based services and the internet of things.

15 Many Japanese firms are so much in need of non-Japanese talent that they have relaxed their normal Japanese-language requirements. One prominent example is Rakuten, which began to hire non-Japanese engineers in large numbers since making English its official language.

20 Working as a software engineer in Japan can be exciting, with the opportunity to get involved in the core of a company's business in a way that is sometimes difficult for non-Japanese in other fields. The diversity can be exhilarating, as many workplaces have non-Japanese staff from a variety of countries, turning them into mini-United
25 Nations of a sort.

(*The Japan Times* 一部抜粋)

＊ Ministry of Economy, Trade and Industry「経済産業省」

sufficient「十分な」

comprise ~「〜を構成する」

project ~「〜を予測する」

face ~「〜に直面する」
deficit「不足」
well-positioned「良い位置を占める」

requirement「要件」

official language「公用語」

diversity「多様性」
exhilarating「楽しい」

of a sort「同種の」

■ Comprehension

Choose two statements that are true about the passage.

1. There are more than 30,000 non-Japanese engineers working in the IT field.
2. The proportion of non-Japanese IT engineers is very low now.
3. In the future, Japan will be short of software engineers.
4. The reason for the shortage of IT engineers is different from that in other fields.
5. Currently, there are enough engineers in the field of software-based technologies.

■ Further Activity

以下のある企業の採用要件に<u>述べられていないもの</u>を一つ選びましょう。

Requirements

- Knowledge of SQL and Python – any other languages would be a plus (BASH, Go, Scala)
- Ability to present data in a simple way using a variety of tools
- Excellent communication (both written and verbal) and interpersonal skills

---

1. 多言語を話す能力
2. 簡潔にデータを発表できる能力
3. 優れた文書作成能力
4. 優れた対人関係能力

chapter 10 ハエの力で食糧危機を解決

Warm-up 1

音声を聴いて、写真（ある研究者が、ウジ虫〈maggot〉が、家畜の排泄物〈livestock feces〉を分解して肥料〈fertilizer〉に変えるシステムを紹介している）を説明している英文を a 〜 c から選びましょう。

© The Asahi Shimbun

a. ☐

b. ☐

c. ☐

Warm-up 2

音声を聴いて 1 〜 10 の（　　）内に当てはまる動詞を書き入れ、写真のシステムに関連する表現を完成しましょう。

1. （　　　　　　　） livestock feces 「家畜の排泄物を分解する」
2. （　　　　　　　） 〜 into fertilizer 「〜を肥料に変える」
3. （　　　　　　　） global hunger 「世界の飢餓を解決する」
4. （　　　　　　　） a self-sufficient system 「自給自足のシステムを考え出す」
5. （　　　　　　　） conflicts 「紛争を終わらせる」
6. （　　　　　　　） over the project 「プロジェクトを引き継ぐ」
7. （　　　　　　　） feces 「排泄物を処理する」
8. （　　　　　　　） food self-sufficiency 「食物の自給自足を実現する」
9. （　　　　　　　） outcomes 「成果を検証する」
10. （　　　　　　　） necessary costs 「必要経費をまかなう」

Warm-up
3

問A、Bに答えましょう。

問
A

音声（前ページの写真で紹介されているウジ虫を使ったシステムの作業過程について）を聴いて、以下の日本語中に数字を書き入れましょう。

1．まず1トンの家畜の排泄物の上にハエの卵を（　　　）グラムばらまく。

2．その卵からかえるウジ虫は（　　　）キログラムである。

3．ウジ虫は（　　　）週間で、排泄物を分解して（　　　）キログラムの肥料に変える。

4．その後、ウジ虫は家畜の飼料となる。

問
B

以下の英文（ウジ虫を利用したシステムの効果について）を読み、質問に答えましょう。

Farmers and universities verified the positive outcomes of the research, reporting that their vegetables grew in size and quality with the fertilizers, and that their livestock became more immune to disease and stress, thanks to the maggot food. And local residents near the new factory need not worry about any nuisance neighbors, as Kushima has implemented full-scale preparations for preventing flies from leaving the premises.

(*The Asahi Shimbun*)

 Notes **immune to ~** 「～に免疫がある」 **nuisance** 「迷惑な」 **Kushima** 「串間氏（本システムの開発者である写真の男性）」 **premise** 「施設」

Which of the following statements is true about Kushima's system?

a. It had a positive effect on vegetables.
b. It failed to make livestock healthy.
c. The local residents regard it as troublesome.
d. Kushima sometimes had to stop its process because flies took flight.

■ Reading

Flies can solve the global food crisis, says researcher

TSUNO, Miyazaki Prefecture — Mitsutaka Kushima is creating a buzz with his novel solution for the global food crisis — flies.

The 41-year-old studied the insects here and devised a self-sufficient system that can transform livestock feces into fertilizer by using fly eggs, then use the resulting maggots as feed.

Kushima believes the system will help solve global hunger and even prevent war. "I want to make people eat to their hearts' content to end conflicts," said Kushima. He will soon start building a factory where 100 tons of feces can be processed daily.

Born in Miyazaki in the prefecture, Kushima joined Chubu Electric Power Co. after graduating from a technical college. A TV program he watched at the age of 24 changed his life. It showed a major study on flies at risk due to the collapse of the Soviet Union, where the research had been started during the Cold War with the aim of achieving food self-sufficiency in spacecraft.

However, a company in Miyazaki took over the study, and the program fired up Kushima's adventurous and ambitious spirit. Kushima returned to his hometown and helped with the research for over a dozen years. Eventually he took charge of the project four years ago when the company president passed away.

Determined not to let the flies in the study die out after over 1,000 generations of the insects had been produced since the former Soviet Union era, Kushima devoted himself to the project, repeatedly incurring debts to cover necessary costs for an air-conditioning system to protect the flies as well as labor.

He lived in fear while being hounded by his creditors. "But I would have died for the flies," said Kushima. His luck changed when a venture company invested in the project, allowing the studies to continue.

(*The Asahi Shimbun* 一部抜粋)

Notes

create a buzz「噂になる」
novel「新しい」

feed「餌」

to their hearts' content
「思う存分」

collapse「崩壊」

eventually「ついには」

determine「決心する」

devote oneself to ~「~に熱中する」
incur debts「借金をする」

hound ~「~にしつこく追われる」

invest「投資する」

■ Comprehension

Choose two statements that are true about the passage.

1. The maggots Kushima grows will become the staple of the human diet.
2. According to Kushima, his system will contribute to solving global hunger.
3. A TV program prompted Kushima to become interested with flies.
4. Kushima started his own project of growing 1,000 flies.
5. Kushima never suffered from a lack of funds for his project.

■ Further Activity

以下は、串間氏が設立した企業 MUSCA（社名の MUSCA はイエバエの英語名 Musca domestica からとったもの）のホームページに掲載されている表です。表を説明しているものを 1 〜 4 から選びましょう。

Measures Against Environmental Problems

	Traditional	MUSCA System
Time Taken for Composting	2-3 months	1 week
Generation of Fermentation Gas	a lot	little
Bad Smell	Yes	none
Groundwater Pollution	Yes	none
Release of Nitrogen	Yes	none
Influence of Outside Temperature	Yes	none

https://musca.info/en/company.php

1. MUSCA システムでは発酵ガスの発生はない。
2. 堆肥化にかかる時間は、従来のシステムに比べて MUSCA システムの方が短い。
3. MUSCA システムでは悪臭を発するのが唯一の欠点である。
4. 両システムとも、地下水汚染や窒素発生などの環境汚染が懸念されている。

chapter

11

社会・医療

やめられない、とまらない！

 51

Warm-up
1

音声を聴いて、写真（依存症の専門医樋口進氏）を説明している英文を a
〜 c から選びましょう。

©KYODO NEWS

a. ❏

b. ❏

c. ❏

 52

Warm-up
2

音声を聴いて、1 〜 10 の下線部に適当な文字を書き入れて単語を完成し
ましょう。

1. ad＿＿＿＿＿＿＿＿＿　　　　「依存症者」

2. ad＿＿＿＿＿＿＿＿＿　　　　「依存症」

3. pre- e＿＿＿＿＿＿＿＿＿　　　「卓越した」

4. ob＿＿＿＿＿＿＿＿＿　　　　「執着」

5. vul＿＿＿＿＿＿＿＿＿　　　　「影響を受けやすい」

6. scour＿＿＿＿＿＿＿＿＿　　　「悩みの種」

7. ne＿＿＿＿＿＿＿＿＿　　　　「おろそかにする、軽視する」

8. path＿＿＿＿＿＿＿＿＿　　　「病理」

9. hy＿＿＿＿＿＿＿＿＿　　　　「衛生状態」

10. yea＿＿＿＿＿＿＿＿＿　　　　「切望する」

Warm-up 3 問 A、B に答えましょう。

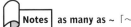 音声（インターネット依存症に関するある報告書について）を聴いて、述べられているものはどれか、1 〜 4 から選びましょう。

1．これは 2018 年の経済産業省の報告書である。

2．930 万人もの中高生がインターネット依存症になっていると述べられている。

3．述べられている数字には大学生も含まれている。

4．インターネット利用は現実逃避と結びついていることが多いと報告されている。

 Notes as many as ~「〜もの」 escapism「現実逃避」

 以下の英文（依存症の専門医樋口進医師の見解について）を読み、質問に答えましょう。

While boys tend to get hooked on shooter and role-playing games, girls are more prone to social media addiction, Higuchi explained. Of the 1,800 people who are admitted to his internet addiction outpatient program every year, 90 percent are gamers, most of them male.

It is easier for him to convince "mild" addicts that their minds can be rewired for long-term gains in the real world, while those with more severe levels of addiction will want to go back to their online reality in pursuit of immediate rewards in the form of dopamine.

(*KYODO NEWS*)

 Notes get hooked on ~「〜に夢中になる」 shooter「シューティングゲーム」 be prone to ~「〜になりやすい」 admit to ~「〜に受け入れる」 outpatient「外来の」 be rewired for ~「〜に向かわせる」 reward「報酬」 in the form of ~「〜という形で」

Which of the following statements is true about in the passage?

a. The annual number of patients who are accepted for Higuchi's internet addiction outpatient program

b. The total number of gamers in Japan

c. The easiest way to overcome internet addiction

d. The importance of families for getting their children back to normal

■ Reading

 55 ## Doctor helps problem gamers looking to hit reset button

TOKYO — How much gaming is too much? This is the question Japan's preeminent addiction expert, Dr. Susumu Higuchi, is trying to answer as he treats people whose lives have been destroyed by video game addiction.

5　Online gaming addiction has become the fastest-growing form of addiction in the 21st century, and it is the most vulnerable people — children— who mainly fall prey to its psychoactive effects, Higuchi says. As head of the Kurihama Medical and Addiction Center in Kanagawa Prefecture, which started the country's first program for
10　internet addition in 2011, Higuchi is rolling up his sleeves to tackle a scourge that has eaten into the vitals of our society.

"This isn't just about Japan, it's happening all over the world," Higuchi said in a recent interview. "We deal with patients every day and see how gaming addiction is only getting worse. How can we
15　ignore that?"

Every Tuesday, the 74-year-old doctor and his two physician colleagues hold sessions for patients whose obsession with games has led them to neglect real-life responsibilities, including family, friends, school, work, and even hygiene, sleeping and eating.

20　The majority are teenage boys brought to the clinic by worried families, but there are also adult men who seek help for gaming habits that have turned from passion to pathology, making them yearn for just one more hit, one more level.

"We're losing money by doing this," Higuchi said of his program
25　at the clinic, where he can take no more than 20 patients a day and each may need years of treatment.

（KYODO NEWS　一部抜粋）

*Kurihama Medical and Addiction Center　「久里浜医療センター」

vulnerable「影響を受けやすい」
fall prey to ~「～の虜になる」
psychoactive effects「精神活性作用」

roll up one's sleeves「本気で取り組む」
tackle ~「～に取り組む」
eat into ~「～に食い込む」
vital「核心部」

physician「医師」
colleague「同僚」

habit「癖」
passion「熱中」

■ Comprehension

Choose two statements that are true about the passage.

1. Dr. Higuchi treats patients suffering from online gaming addiction.
2. This kind of addiction problem is happening only in Japan.
3. The clinic that Dr. Higuchi works for is located in Chiba Prefecture.
4. He and his colleagues hold sessions for patients about how to neglect personal problems.
5. It may take years for patients to overcome addiction.

■ Further Activity

以下の（　　　）内の語句を並び替え、樋口医師へのインタビューを完成しましょう。

©iStock.com/takasuu

Interviewer: (**1.** it / internet addiction / makes / difficult / to treat / What)?

Dr. Higuchi: A person can abstain from alcohol and be in a zero state, but you can't do that with the internet. You can't unplug from technology entirely.

Interviewer: What complicates matters is that many game addicts actually believe (**2.** into / turn / a career / their hobby / they / can).

Dr. Higuchi: Game-makers are knowingly turning customers into addicts. They will keep getting smarter so they can steal all of the players' waking hours and enslave them to their games. The fight will continue.

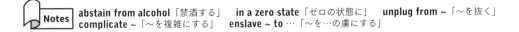

Notes **abstain from alcohol**「禁酒する」 **in a zero state**「ゼロの状態に」 **unplug from ~**「～を抜く」
complicate ~「～を複雑にする」 **enslave ~ to** …「～を…の虜にする」

chapter

12

科学

受験生に朗報？

Warm-up 1

音声を聴いて、イラスト（マウスの脳内の嗅周皮質〈perirhinal cortex〉の位置を示している）を説明する英文を a〜c から選びましょう。

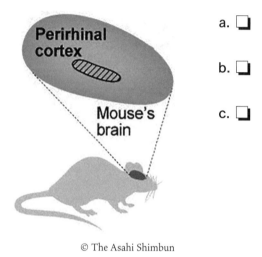

© The Asahi Shimbun

a. ☐

b. ☐

c. ☐

Warm-up 2

並列的に物事を述べる際に使われる and, but, as well as などは、動詞なら動詞、名詞なら名詞、文なら文同士を結びます。音声を聞いて（　　）内に当てはまる語を書き入れ、以下の 1〜3 の並列構造の英文を完成しましょう。

1．The finding could help （　　　　　　） the mechanism of remembering as well as （　　　　　　） drugs to treat Alzheimer's disease.

この発見は、アルツハイマー病の治療薬の開発だけでなく、記憶のメカニズムを解明する助けとなる可能性がある。

2．Histamine is involved in learning and memories as well as （　　　　　　） and （　　　　　　）.

ヒスタミンは、睡眠や目覚めだけでなく、学習や記憶にも関与している。

3．Rodents have a habit of taking interest, through （　　　　　　） and （　　　　　　）, in new objects.

ねずみには触覚と嗅覚で新しい物に興味を持つ習性がある。

Warm-up
3 問 A、B に答えましょう。

58 問 **A** 音声を聴いて、嗅周皮質と記憶の関係の研究に関して述べられているのはどれか、1 〜 4 から選びましょう。

1．嗅周皮質は物を確認したり覚えたりするときに機能する。

2．ある研究ではヒスタミンを出す物質を特定した。

3．ある研究ではヒスタミンが脳全体を活性化することが分かった。

4．ある研究ではヒスタミンの放出を抑えたら長期記憶がよくなることが分かった。

 Note | activate ~「〜を活性化する」

59 問 **B** 以下の英文を読み、本文の内容に合うように質問に答えましょう。

A research team asked the male and female participants to take histamine-activating drugs and tested them on their memory of images they had seen a week before. Those who had taken the histamine-boosting drug were able to remember the images much more easily, with a success rate several percentage points higher than those in the group that had not taken the drugs. The rate of correct answers especially improved for questions at a higher level of difficulty.

(*The Asahi Shimbun*)

 Notes | **histamine-activating**「ヒスタミンを活性化する」 **boost ~**「〜を高める、増やす」

Which of the following statements is true about the study?

a. The participants took the histamine-reducing drug before they were tested.

b. The researchers tested the participants on whether they could remember the images.

c. The amount of histamine increased in those who had not taken the drug.

d. The people who took the drug had difficulty in remembering the images.

■ Reading

How do we remember memories we have forgotten?

Japanese scientists improved long-term memory in subjects by activating histamine in the brain, a finding that could help unveil the mechanism of remembering as well as develop drugs to treat Alzheimer's disease.

5　　The study by a research team, comprising scientists of Hokkaido University and the University of Tokyo, was published in the official journal of the Society of Biological Psychiatry, on Jan. 8.

Over time, memories slowly fade and are eventually forgotten. However, traces of them are believed to remain in the brain.

10　Histamine, a substance released in allergic reactions, is also involved in learning and memories as well as sleep and wakefulness.

As anti-histamine drugs reduce the performance of remembering, it is believed that if the central nervous system that releases and receives histamine, which functions as neurotransmitters in the brain,
15　can be sufficiently activated, forgotten memories can be retrieved.

The study team thus investigated how the histamine-boosting drug affected memory performance in mice and humans through experiments. In the experiments with mice, the scientists placed two identical objects in a box with a mouse, and then replaced one of them
20　with a different object.

Rodents have a habit of taking interest, through touch and smell, in new objects, meaning that if they still remember the objects in the box, they will prefer the newly placed one.

In an initial training session, the mice preferred the new item, but
25　after more than three days, they became unable to distinguish between the two. However, after being administered the drug that boosts histamine in the nervous system, the mice approached the new object even one month after the initial training sessions.

(*The Asahi Shimbun*　一部抜粋)

* the Society of Biological Psychiatry「生物学的精神科医学会」

comprise ~「~から成る」

fade「消えていく」
eventually「最終的には」
trace「痕跡」

release ~「~を放出する」
allergic「アレルギーの」

central nervous system
「中枢神経」
neurotransmitter「神経伝達物質」
retrieve ~「~を回復する」

identical「同じ」

rodent「齧歯類、ねずみ」

initial「初めの」

distinguish ~「~を区別する」
administer ~「~を投与する」

■ Comprehension

Choose two statements that are true about the passage.

1. Histamine makes it easier for people to forget memories.
2. Histamine is related to learning and memorizing.
3. It is believed that if the central nervous system can be sufficiently activated, forgotten memories can be recovered.
4. The study team investigated the effectiveness of the histamine-boosting drug for improving performance in the workplace.
5. The mice, which were given the drug, remembered the objects in the box and preferred the older object.

■ Further Activity

以下の図の空所内に当てはまる適当な語句を選択肢から選んで書き入れ、図の説明を完成しましょう。

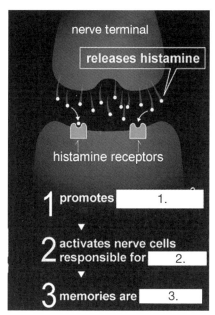

nerve terminal

releases histamine

histamine receptors

1 promotes ___1.___

2 activates nerve cells responsible for ___2.___

3 memories are ___3.___

© The Asahi Shimbun

| histamine release | recovered | memories |

13 デジタル格差をなくしたい

61

Warm-up 1

音声（ケニアに配備された高高度気球について）を聴いて、写真を説明している英文を a ～ c から選びましょう。

Source : Loon.

a. ☐

b. ☐

c. ☐

62

Warm-up 2

意味を参考にして（　　）内に前置詞を書き入れ、音声を聞いて答えを確認しましょう。

1．result（　　　　　）～　　　　　　　　　　「～の結果となる」

2．choose A（　　　　　）B　　　　　　　　　「A を B として選ぶ」

3．regions devastated（　　　　　）hurricanes 「ハリケーンに破壊された地域」

4．be linked（　　　　）～　　　　　　　　　「～につながっている」

5．a lack（　　　　）～　　　　　　　　　　「～の不足」

6．due（　　　　）～　　　　　　　　　　　「～のために」

7．（　　　　）emergencies　　　　　　　　「災害時に」

8．fit（　　　　）the company's policies　　「企業の方針に合う」

9．graduate（　　　　）～　　　　　　　　　「～から卒業する／巣立つ」

10．mark a milestone（　　　　）～　　　　「～において画期的出来事となる」

音声を聴いて、話題となっている人々が住んでいる地域として述べられているものを選びましょう。

1．ネット接続ができない地域

2．インフラが整っている地域

3．人口が密集している地域

4．自然環境が過酷な地域

以下の英文（「デジタル格差」をなくすことに挑戦しているフェイスブック社の試みについて）を読み、質問に答えましょう。

　　Facebook has been trying to deliver the internet via solar-powered drones. Last year, it completed a test flight above Arizona, after an earlier flight resulted in a crash. But last month, Facebook announced it would stop making its own aircraft and would support other high-altitude connectivity initiatives.

(AP)

Notes **deliver ~**「～を提供する」　　**connectivity**「（インターネットとの）接続性」　　**initiative**「新たな試み」

Which of the following statements is true about Facebook's project?

a. Arizona was chosen as the test site of the project last year.
b. Every trial of the project has been successful so far.
c. Facebook has a plan to fly drones next month.
d. Their project will be supported by other projects using drones.

■ Reading

High-altitude balloons to deliver internet access in Kenya

MOUNTAIN VIEW, Calif. (AP) — Loon, a Google-affiliated company, has chosen Kenya as the home of its first announced commercial deal for delivering internet access to hard-to-reach areas using high-altitude balloons.

5　　Loon, which is linked to Google through parent company Alphabet Inc., says it will work with Telkom Kenya to deliver 4G/LTE cellular access to Kenya in 2019. Many people there still are not connected to the internet because of a lack of infrastructure to support it.

The balloons will be tested in central Kenya, which has been

10　difficult to service due to mountainous or inaccessible terrain. The high-altitude balloons have already been deployed in emergencies in Peru and Puerto Rico, where they helped regions devastated by floods and hurricanes.

Since Google first launched the project in 2013, its goal has been to

15　connect everyone on the planet. While getting more people connected fits with Google's ambitions of making information "universally accessible and useful," it also increases the number of people who can use Google's ad-supported services.

The announcement comes just a week after Loon graduated from

20　Alphabet's secretive "moonshot factory" known as X. That means it is considered a full-fledged company beside sibling companies including Google and self-driving car developer Waymo.

"We're excited to take a big step forward for our business and mission," Loon CEO Alastair Westgarth, said in a Medium post.

25　Westgarth says Alphabet marks a significant milestone in a journey that began in 2013 when a New Zealand sheep farmer became one of the first to connect with Loon test balloons.

(AP　一部抜粋)

＊ Loon「(プロジェクト・) ルーン／ルーン社」とは、旧グーグル X 社が革新的なアイデアを育てるために始めた「ムーンショットファクトリー」プロジェクトの一つ。後にグーグル社は、組織再編を実施し、親会社であるアルファベット社の元で、両プロジェクトは、独立企業ルーン社と X 社となった。

Notes

affiliated company「姉妹会社」

commercial deal「商用提供」

mountainous or inaccessible terrain「山岳地帯や接近不可能な地形」

ambition「野望」
universally「一般に」

ad-supported「広告支援の」

secretive「秘密主義の」

full-fledged「一人前の」

Medium「メディアム (Loon 社のブログ)」
post「投稿」

■ Comprehension

Choose two statements that are true about the passage.

1. The parent company of Loon is Alphabet Inc.
2. The first commercial balloons have been deployed in Peru and Puerto Rico.
3. Loon was once one of the projects launched by Google.
4. Google wants to part from Alphabet's projects.
5. The first test balloons of Loon were launched in Kenya.

■ Further Activity

以下は、ルーン社のブログ「メディアム」の、ブログのコンセプトと会員入会の方法について述べた英文からの抜粋です。述べられているものを１～４から選びましょう。

Our story

Medium taps into the brains of the world's most insightful writers, thinkers, and storytellers to bring you the smartest takes on topics that matter. So whatever your interest, you can always find fresh thinking and unique perspectives.

Membership

Become a Medium member for $5/month or $50/year and get unlimited access to the smartest writers and biggest ideas you won't find anywhere else.

---

https://medium.com/about
https://medium.com/membership

1. ブログは、ルーン社社員のアイデアを披露している。
2. ブログ会員になる人は、科学技術の知識を持っていなければならない。
3. 会員は、月ごとに会費を払わねばならない。
4. 会費を払えば、ブログ内の情報には無制限にアクセスできる。

健康
ホラー動画で PR

Warm-up 1

音声を聴いて、写真（佐賀県歯科医師会の PR 動画の一場面）を説明している英文を a ～ c から選びましょう。

歯の間に汚れがつまりやすくなるので
むし歯になるリスクが高くなります。

提供：一般社団法人佐賀県歯科医師会／株式会社佐賀広告センター

a. ☐

b. ☐

c. ☐

Warm-up 2

1 ～ 6 は現在分詞（V-ing）と過去分詞（V-ed）が、単独の場合は修飾する名詞の前につき、他の語句を伴う場合は後ろから名詞を修飾する例です。現在分詞の意味と過去分詞の意味の違いに気をつけ、音声を聴き（　　　）内に当てはまる語を書き取りましょう。

1．behind an（　　　　　　）dentist 「何も気づいていない歯医者の後ろで」

2．a video（　　　　　　）a zombie 「ゾンビを主役にしているビデオ」

3．（　　　　　　）teeth 「腐りかけている歯」

4．a fairy（　　　　　　）in white 「白装束の妖精」

5．a dentist（　　　　　　）interviewed 「インタビューされている歯科医」

6．an（　　　　　　）way 「前例のないやり方」

3　問 A、B に答えましょう。

 音声を聴いて、佐賀県歯科医師会が作成したビデオに登場する女性の歯の妖精「サバコ」について述べられているものを選びましょう。

1. 彼女は、ホラー小説の主人公と同じ名前である。

2. 彼女の名前の漢字表記は「佐歯子」である。

3. 彼女は、有名人の名前をもじって自身に名前をつけた。

4. 彼女が誕生したのは、1991 年である。

 以下の英文を読み、本文の内容に合うように英文を完成しましょう。

　　The younger dentists insisted on the unprecedented way of using a zombie and a fairy character to promote oral hygiene, arguing that the dental association would lose its value if it failed to draw the attention of youngsters. Although questions had been raised on whether having the undead and the spooky sprite represent the association was a good idea, the characters appear to be having an effect.

(The Asahi Shimbun)

 Notes | **oral hygiene**「口腔衛生」　**spooky spite**「薄気味悪い妖精」

According to the passage,

a. the association would lose its reputation by using a zombie for promotion.
b. the association has already failed to draw the attention of young people.
c. using a zombie character is a good idea to promote dental health.
d. the zombie character seems to have some kind of impact.

■ Reading

Zombie, creepy tooth fairy scare Saga children to brush their teeth

SAGA — A zombie frustratingly tries to pick food, perhaps a piece of brain, from his teeth, while a creepy fairy hovers menacingly behind an unsuspecting dentist. These monsters are the new symbols in the Saga Prefectural Dental Association's campaign to get residents
5 to brush their teeth.

Special make-up transforms a dentist into a zombie who stares into the video camera and shows his horribly misaligned and rotting teeth. The message is clear: people with irregular teeth should undergo orthodontic treatment before tooth decay sets in.

10 The tooth fairy, called "Sabako," does not actually give money in exchange for baby teeth. Instead, she wears a white outfit and allows her long black hair to hang over her face.

In one video, she comically brushes her teeth with a green toothbrush and uses orange dental floss. She urges viewers to brush
15 their teeth immediately after eating to remove food debris and plaque.

In another video, the fairy dressed in white suddenly appears behind a dentist being interviewed and screams her signature phrase: "Ha" (teeth). "Sabako" is played by Ayumi Sonoda, a member of local idol group Pinky Sky. Although her hair covers her face, her shiny
20 white grin can be seen.

Naoki Miyazoe, director of Saga Ad Center, said the horror-themed videos have proved immensely popular online. "I think our promotional video clips leave a powerful lasting impression on the viewer's mind," he said.

25 "We want people to understand that they can live a long healthy life if they learn to take care of their teeth by watching the videos," said Takaharu Terao, chairman of the association.

(*The Asahi Shimbun* 一部抜粋)

creepy「薄気味悪い」

frustratingly「イライラして」
pick ~「~をほじくって取る」
menacingly「脅すように」

misaligned「歯並びの悪い」

orthodontic「歯列矯正の」
tooth decay「虫歯」

debris「カス」
plaque「歯垢」

signature phrase「決めぜりふ」

immensely「非常に」

■ Comprehension

Choose two statements that are true about the passage.

1. In a video, the undead and a fairy are eating a piece of brain.
2. A dentist has become very popular in the zombie video.
3. One of the causes of tooth decay is misaligned teeth.
4. "Sabako" makes an appearance silently in the videos.
5. According to Miyazoe, people like to watch the horror-themed videos online.

■ Further Activity

次の文章（県民の注意を引くためのある工夫）を読んで、「サガケンシカイシカイ」を漢字で表記しましょう。

The association used puns such as "Sabako" to appeal to a wider audience. Similarly, the kanji character "kai" that means "horror" replaced another kanji character with the same pronunciation but meaning "association," as in "Saga ken Shikaishi kai" (Saga Prefecture Dental Association), in the videos.

(*The Asahi Shimbun* 一部改変)

漢字表記 （   ）

そのため食事をした後はすぐに
歯磨きで歯垢を取り除きましょう。

提供：一般社団法人佐賀県歯科医師会／株式会社佐賀広告センター

「新しい石油」の争奪合戦

71
Warm-up **1**

音声を聴いて、グラフを説明している英文を a 〜 c から選びましょう。

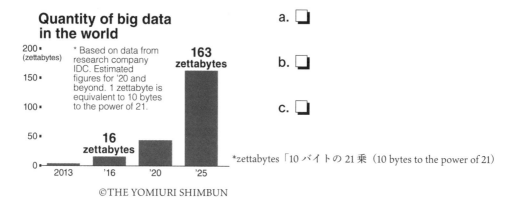

Quantity of big data in the world

200 (zettabytes)

* Based on data from research company IDC. Estimated figures for '20 and beyond. 1 zettabyte is equivalent to 10 bytes to the power of 21.

150

100

50

16 zettabytes

163 zettabytes

0

2013   '16   '20   '25

©THE YOMIURI SHIMBUN

a. ☐

b. ☐

c. ☐

*zettabytes「10 バイトの 21 乗（10 bytes to the power of 21)

72
Warm-up **2**

1 〜 10 の動詞に接尾辞 (-ment, -ion) を加えて抽象名詞を作り、音声を聴いて答えを確認しましょう。また、それぞれの抽象名詞の意味を a 〜 j から選びましょう。

1. develop （　　　）
2. inform （　　　）
3. improve （　　　）
4. succeed （　　　）
5. administer （　　　）
6. protect （　　　）
7. transact （　　　）
8. regulate （　　　）
9. operate （　　　）
10. revitalize （　　　）

a. 連続
b. 規制
c. 運営
d. 再生
e. 整備／改善
f. 情報
g. 発展／開発
h. 取引
i. 政権
j. 保護

Warm-up 3

問 A、B に答えましょう。

問 A

音声（データ保護主義をとる中国について）を聴いて、以下の文中の空所に適当な数字を書き入れましょう。

中国は、（**1.**　　　　）年までに、世界のデータの（**2.**　　　　）パーセントを占める容量を手にすると思われている。この時点で、中国はデータ保有量が世界（**3.**　　　　）位となる。経済価値は、（**4.**　　　　）元—日本円で（**5.**　　　　）円を越えるだろうと言われている。

問 B

以下の英文（「新しい石油」獲得のための中国の戦略について）を読んで、以下の質問に答えましょう。

Big data is a data resource, such as individuals' online browsing and purchase histories, referred to as "the new oil." Chinese President Xi Jinping aims to build a powerful country that will rival the United States by the middle of the 21st century. With an eye toward the development of a "digital China," he is poised to battle the United States for control of these data resources. The Chinese government is establishing big data pilot zones for such purposes as research and development and the improvement of big data-related infrastructure.

(*The Japan News*)

 Notes | be poised to ~「～する構えである」　**pilot zone**「試験範囲」

Which of the following statements is true about the passage?

a. Big data refers to online data analyzing oil resources.

b. According to Chinese President Xi, the United States gets big data to itself.

c. Xi's ambition is to control the digital resources.

d. The pilot zones established by China include entertainment.

■ Reading

China strengthening digital protectionism

In response to the succession of protectionist trade policies issued by U.S. President Donald Trump, Chinese President Xi Jinping has cast himself as a defender of free trade. However, he has actually promoted digital protectionism, in which China has tightly managed
5　the distribution of big data. Xi's administration is in the process of walling off big data to achieve its goals. The country's Cybersecurity Law, which was enforced in June 2017, plays a central role in this policy.

Under the pretexts of "national security" and "protection of
10　personal information," the law requires, in principle, companies that collect personal information and other important data within China to save such data on servers in China.

If a company wishes to transfer data outside of the country, the transaction must first be reviewed by the authorities. Limits are
15　imposed on the transfer of information across the country's borders. It is thought that the impact of the law will inevitably extend to foreign-owned companies, including Japanese firms.

In May, the European Union enacted its own General Data Protection Regulation, which obliges companies to maintain controls
20　on personal information. Although there are concerns about the possible detrimental effects of excessively strict regulations, the prevailing view in Japanese business circles is that the EU regulations differ in intent from those of China. According to this view, the EU aims to protect the human rights of individuals, while China
25　emphasizes strengthened regulations and its operations are regarded as opaque.

It is natural that governments and other institutions around the world have heightened their vigilance in response to China's Cybersecurity Law, viewing it as a trade barrier that will serve to
30　exclude foreign companies.

Akira Amari, former minister in charge of economic revitalization, says China's Cybersecurity Law is a system of one-way traffic.

In partnership with Europe and the United States, Japan has spearheaded voluntary meetings on digital trade at the World Trade
35　Organization, in hopes that formulating rules will ensure the free movement of data and ban the forced transfer of technology.

(*The Japan News* 一部抜粋)

Notes

a succession of ~「相次ぐ～」

cast ~ as ...「～に…の役割を与える」
defender「擁護者」

wall off ~「～を囲い込む」
enforce ~「～を施行する」

under a pretext of ~「～にかこつけて」

transfer ~「～を送信する」
authorities「当局」
impose on ~「～に課する」
inevitably「必然的に」

oblige「義務づける」

detrimental effect「弊害」
prevailing「一般的な」
intent「意図」

opaque「不透明な」

vigilance「警戒」

exclude ~「～を除外する」

spearhead ~「～を先導する」
formulate ~「～を策定する」

■ Comprehension

Choose two statements that are true about the passage.

1. Donald Trump regards Xi Jinping as a defender of free trade.
2. The Trump administration put the Cybersecurity Law into force to protect the US from China.
3. Foreign-owned companies will be free of the influence of the Cybersecurity Law.
4. According to Japanese business circles, the EU's rules aim to protect human rights.
5. The Japanese government wants to promote the free transfer of data.

■ Further Activity

以下の図を見て、中国はデジタル保護主義を下記の 1 ～ 4 のどれを利用して広めようとしているかを選びましょう。

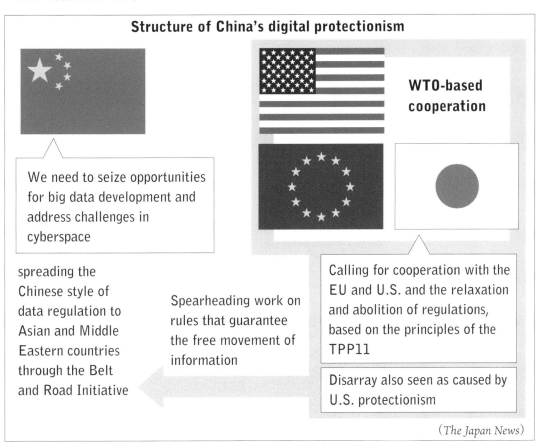

Structure of China's digital protectionism

WTO-based cooperation

We need to seize opportunities for big data development and address challenges in cyberspace

spreading the Chinese style of data regulation to Asian and Middle Eastern countries through the Belt and Road Initiative

Spearheading work on rules that guarantee the free movement of information

Calling for cooperation with the EU and U.S. and the relaxation and abolition of regulations, based on the principles of the TPP11

Disarray also seen as caused by U.S. protectionism

(*The Japan News*)

1. 「一帯一路」政策
2. 世界貿易機関
3. 環太平洋パートナーシップ協定
4. アメリカの保護貿易主義

編著者

深山晶子（みやま　あきこ）

大阪工業大学名誉教授

村尾純子（むらお　じゅんこ）

大阪工業大学

ソーシャル・アウトルック
—メディア英語で社会を視る

2020 年 2 月 20 日　第 1 版発行
2024 年 3 月 20 日　第 6 版発行

編 著 者──深山晶子
　　　　　　村尾純子

発 行 者──前田俊秀

発 行 所──株式会社 三修社

〒 150-0001 東京都渋谷区神宮前 2-2-22
TEL03-3405-4511　FAX03-3405-4522
振替 00190-9-72758
https://www.sanshusha.co.jp
編集担当　菊池 暁

印 刷 所──広研印刷株式会社

©2020 Printed in Japan　ISBN978-4-384-33493-7 C1082

表紙デザイン　──峯岸孝之（Comix Brand）
本文 DTP　　──川原田良一
音声収録・製作──ELEC ／高速録音株式会社
ナレーター　　──Rachel Walzer, Chris Koprowski

教科書準拠 CD 発売
本書の準拠 CD をご希望の方は弊社までお問い合わせください。